# editorial

September 2005

The first report by the Centre for Public Inquiry concerns the decision by the local authority in County Meath to permit the construction of a four storey hotel beside Trim Castle, one of Ireland's most important national monuments. The report is the result of complaints to this office by elected representatives in County Meath and concerned citizens including members of the heritage protection organisation, An Taisce. The investigation raises several issues of significant public concern which are outlined in detail in the following pages. The report has been made available to the Minister for the Environment, Heritage and Local Government, Dick Roche, members of the Oireachtas and of the relevant local authorities as well as to a large number of interested parties including the people of Trim.

PUE

# contents

Written by: Frank Connolly
Research: Denise Clare
Photography: Derek Speirs
Photographs of *Braveheart* set by the late Trevor Looney
Design: Public Communications Centre
Printed by: Hudson Killeen

Published by;
Centre for Public Inquiry-Fiosrú an Phobail
The Courtyard, 25 Great Strand Street, Dublin 1
Tel; 01 8748851    Fax; 01 8748976
E mail info@publicinquiry.ie
Website; www.publicinquiry.ie

## MAP OF TRIM

showing Trim Castle, the hotel development site
and previous land owners.

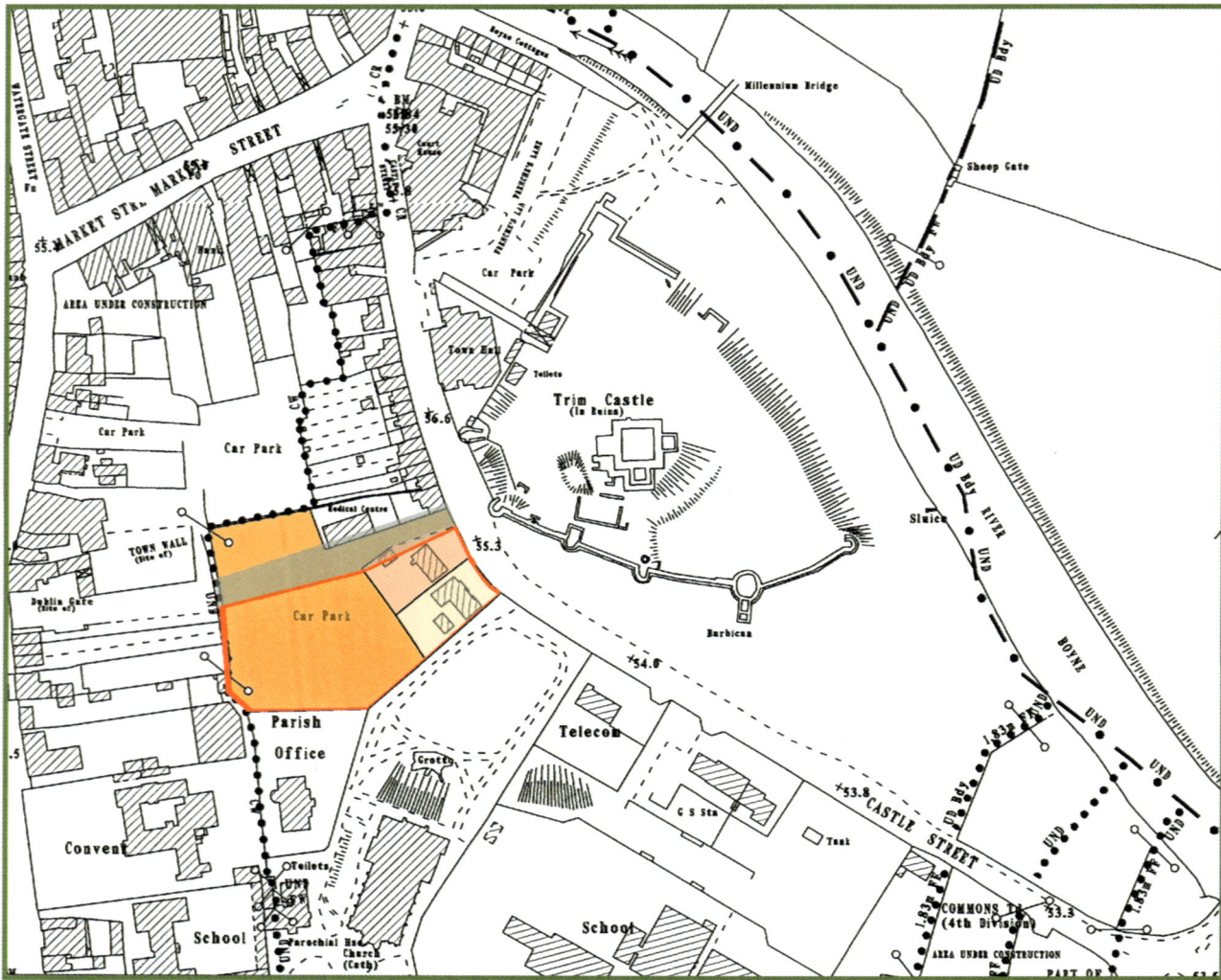

Scale:— 1:2500
Scála:— 1:2500

| 100 | 50 | 0 | | 100 Metres |

| 200 | 100 | 0 | | 200 Feet |

| Legend | |
|---|---|
| ▬▬▬ Hotel Development Site | ▮ Nun's Garden |
| ▨▨▨ Proposed Road | ▮ Paul Gilroy |
| | ▮ Ms Sheila Kealey |

In an extraordinary tale of alleged intrigue within the local council and a failure by central government to protect a monument of national and international significance a four storey hotel is being constructed by D. O'Brien Developments Ltd. just yards from the perimeter wall of the recently restored Trim Castle, County Meath.

# TRIM CASTLE

**It survived 800 years of war, rebellion and the ravages of time.
Will it finally be undermined by shocking political decision-making?**

## A LOCAL AND NATIONAL SCANDAL

Following a lengthy investigation and detailed perusal of documents obtained under the Freedom of Information Act the Centre for Public Inquiry has discovered that a number of former and currently serving councillors were advised, against their better judgement, to agree to sell council land, intended for a public car park, to a private developer who was then granted planning permission for the controversial hotel development.

FOI documents have revealed a consistent refusal by the former Minister for the Environment, Martin Cullen, and his close advisers to heed warnings from senior heritage officials in his department who vigorously sought, in a series of detailed correspondence, to lodge an objection to the planning application and then to appeal the decision by the Trim Urban District Council to An Bord Pleanála.

Instead, the minister said that he would seek to have the development scaled back rather than proceed with a formal objection despite warnings that the development was potentially in breach of the National Monuments Act, and by his own senior heritage officials, that it would irreparably damage the Castle.

## SCALING DOWN RESULTS IN A LARGER DEVELOPMENT

After the developer had obtained permission for the hotel he proceeded to lodge a fresh application for additional bedrooms and car parking spaces, which was accepted by An Bord Pleanála who overruled an objection by An Taisce in a decision on June 13, 2005. The end result effectively rubbished the efforts by the minister and his officials to scale back rather than prevent the development as recommended by the senior heritage officials in the department.

The decision has resulted in a development currently under construction which is as large as that intended in the original application which the former minister promised he would have scaled back. Mr David O'Brien whom, with his wife Lynda, is a director of D. O'Brien Developments Ltd is building a 68 bedroom hotel, 400 seat function room, shops bar gymnasium and car parking on the approximately 1.3 acre site. Mr Cullen had faced down efforts by his senior heritage officials to object to the hotel development arguing instead that the project should be "scaled back".

The then chairman, a former councillor and three currently serving members of Trim Urban District Council have claimed that they were pressured into supporting a proposal to sell approximately 1.3 acres of council owned land to the developer for the construction of the hotel within yards of the historic Norman built 12th Century castle.

## HOW THE COUNCIL GOT THE LAND

The land had been acquired from the Sisters of Mercy who agreed to sell what was a former graveyard adjacent to their convent and grounds from which the remains of a number of their deceased members had been exhumed. The nuns agreed to sell the land, now worth several million euro, for some £42,500 (€53,963) when the UDC requested its use for a public car park.

In 1997 the OPW agreed to provide a sum of £50,000 (€63,486) towards the purchase of the land from the nuns and the development of the car park.

In January 1998, the Minister for Arts, Heritage, Gaeltacht and the Islands, Síle de Valera wrote to the then Environment Minister, Noel Dempsey, to confirm that £3 million (€3.8 million) had been allocated to the Trim Castle project from the EU Operational Programme for Tourism 1994-1999, including a sum of £0.05million for car/bus parking.

The use of the funds became the subject of an inquiry initiated by the Minister for the Environment, Dick Roche, shortly after he came into office in September 2004 when it emerged that the land was not being used for a public car parking amenity but had ended up in the hands of a private developer.

## THE COFFEE SHOP THAT NEVER STOOD A CHANCE

A woman who owned another property acquired by the county council on which a portion of the hotel is now being built claims that she was forced to sell only when a compulsory purchase order was mooted in relation to her land.

Ms Sheila Kealey has told the Centre for Public Inquiry that she sought to open a tourism based coffee shop on her site but was told that she would not get planning permission for a commercial development so close to the castle. She sold the site to Meath County Council for £185,000 (€234,901) in 2000. The developer purchased an adjoining site of approximately the same dimensions for more than twice this amount less than two years later.

The nuns agreed to sell the land, now worth several million euro, for some £42,500 (€53,963) when the UDC requested its use for a public car park.

## HOW PUBLIC LAND ENDED UP IN PRIVATE HANDS

Central to the intricate story of how valuable public land, intended to service tourists visiting the castle, ended up in private hands is the role of Oliver Perkins, the now retired Trim Town Council manager and for many years the engineer for Meath County Council.

Having acquired the land from the Sisters of Mercy and Ms Kealey the Town Council advertised, in April 2001, for tenders to develop the site at Castle Street opposite the imposing monument. In June 2001 a bidders conference was held and five developers were interviewed about their proposals for the land.

An advisory panel, which included Dermot Mulligan of architects firm, Newenham Mulligan Associates, the then Meath assistant county manager Joe Crockett, former secretary general of the Department of the Environment, Jimmy Farrelly, and Mr Perkins himself was appointed with agreement by the elected members.

By December 2001 the advisory panel had selected a proposal for a hotel submitted by D. O'Brien Developments Ltd ahead of a proposal presented by the competing tender from local builder, Tom Hora, for a theatre with hostel accommodation which had been earlier recommended as a preferred use in a report commissioned by the council.

A day later, on December 21 2001, Mr O'Brien was informed by letter that his was the preferred proposal for the site and that he should "initiate pre-planning discussions with the planning authority in order to progress the development of the site."

# "I now believe that I was hoodwinked into making a decision to vote in favour of Mr O'Brien's hotel development."

## THE PRESSURE COMES ON STRONG.

When the elected councillors were presented early in 2002 with what appeared to be a fait accompli by the advisory panel a number of councillors including the then chairman, Peter Crinion, and former chairman Phillip Cantwell objected on the grounds that any final decision on such a significant planning matter for the town should have been made by the elected members of the Town Council.

According to council chairman Peter Crinion the elected members were "hoodwinked".

"At a meeting in January 2002 we were told by Mr Perkins that O'Brien had won the tender. The assessment or advisory panel had become an adjudication panel. The discussions became very heated. I now believe that I was hoodwinked into making a decision to vote in favour of Mr O'Brien's hotel development".

The decision to dispose of council land to Mr O'Brien, effectively endorsing the hotel proposal, was passed by six votes to three with Phillip Cantwell among those in opposition. Both Cllr Cantwell and Cllr Jimmy Peppard were equally unhappy with the hotel plan and the potential threat to the integrity of the castle. These members have claimed that they were advised of possible litigation against the council if they ignored the recommendations of the advisory panel. Mr Perkins has said that he has no recollection of any suggestion of the council or councillors being exposed to possible litigation.

Other members, including Cllrs Vincent McHugh and Gerry Reilly, defend the decision in favour of the hotel on the grounds that Trim urgently needed commercial development at the time. The decision by the council to grant planning permission to Mr O'Brien just over a year after these contentious deliberations left the task of objecting to this threat to a national monument to the senior government officials whose job it is to monitor and protect such important heritage structures.

At the signing of contract documents for sale of council land in October 2002 were (from front left) Trim Area Manager Oliver Perkins and David O'Brien, (back) Trim Town Clerk Mary Maguire, Cllr Peter Higgins, Trim Town Council Vice-Chairman Gerry Reilly, Mrs. Lynda O'Brien, Mr. Rory McEntee Council Solicitor and Mr. Patrick Cusack, Cusack McTiernan & Co                    *Meath Chronicle 19/10/02*

## THE MINISTER REPEATEDLY IGNORES HIS SENIOR EXPERTS

But Freedom of Information documents show that the Minister for the Environment, Martin Cullen, and his policy co-ordinator, Feargal O'Coigligh, consistently faced down attempts by architects, archaeologists and heritage officers in his department to stop the development on the grounds of its obtrusive scale and its adverse visual impact on Trim Castle which had been restored at a cost of more than €4.46 million euro to the tax payer over the preceding years.

Dúchas, the Heritage Section of the department wrote numerous letters to the minister setting out its stringent objections to the development before planning permission was granted in August 2003.

Dúchas, in July 2003, advised the minister that it had "consistently expressed concern regarding the scale and bulk of the proposed development which we believe to be inappropriate in this highly sensitive historical location adjacent to Trim Castle a National monument in state care."

Dúchas pointed out that they had met with the development team seeking revisions to the original proposals but that "despite these revisions and subsequent ones it continues to be our opinion that this development due to its scale and bulk would have an adverse and negative impact on the setting and visual appreciation of Trim Castle and a number of protected structures. Consequently we recommend that the planning authority refuse permission for the development as currently proposed."

## MINISTER RECOMMENDS SCALING BACK FACADE

Despite this plea from the senior officials in the department the minister through his policy co-ordinator replied, on July 30, 2003 that "it is considered that the department should not recommend refusal of this development. However it should be recommended that the bulk and scale of the front facade be scaled/stepped back in order not to dominate the appreciation of the Castle."

The hotel development was scaled back from the original proposals of 68 bedrooms to 58 in July 2003.

After planning permission was granted by the local authority in late August 2003 senior officials including the departments' chief archaeologist, Brian Duffy, sought to appeal the permission to An Bord Pleanála in a last ditch effort to register the reservations of the State's leading heritage guardians.

"…it continues to be our opinion that this development due to its scale and bulk would have an adverse and negative impact on the setting and visual appreciation of Trim Castle and a number of protected structures. Consequently we recommend that the planning authority refuse permission for the development as currently proposed."

## HERITAGE EXPERTS' FINAL OBJECTIONS IGNORED

In their letter to An Bord Pleanála of September 16, 2003 Mr Duffy and a senior colleague wrote that "the National Monuments section of this department concurs with the recommendations of the Architectural Heritage Advisory Section and considers that the development due to its scale and bulk will have a negative impact on the setting and visual appreciation of Trim Castle, a National Monument of international significance in State ownership."

In reply, Mr O'Coigligh on behalf of the minister responded that "while concerns may still remain regarding the scale of the development as now revised it is considered that reasonable efforts have been made by the developer and Trim Town Council and an appeal to An Bord Pleanála by the department is not justified in this instance."

## DESPITE TOP-LEVEL CONCERNS, NO OFFICIAL OBJECTION LODGED

Despite the recommendations of the most senior figures charged with protecting the State's heritage no objection was lodged by an official body to the controversial planning permission.

An attempt by a concerned environmentalist who had prepared an historic study of Trim Castle and other monuments was withdrawn, again in controversial circumstances. Mr Dermot Kelly, an inspector with An Bord Pleanála, who lodged his objection in a private capacity, withdrew his appeal after stringent representations to An Bord Pleanála by architects acting for the developer.

## HOTEL PLAN IS SCALED UP

Despite the interventions of Dúchas and the minister's office to achieve the scaling back of the development, Mr O'Brien made an application to the council in 2004 to increase the number of bedrooms from 58 to 70. This was appealed by An Taisce but its objections were overruled by An Bord Pleanála which granted permission for ten extra bedrooms and additional car parking in June last with the result that the minister's aim to have the development scaled back was completely undermined.

Asked what the minister now thought of the controversial development a spokesman for Mr Cullen said – "The minister was advised by his heritage officials at the time and the role he would have played would have been on the back of that advice." In fact an FOI document reveals the minister repeatedly ignored the advice of his heritage officials.

Despite the recommendations of the most senior figures charged with protecting the State's heritage no objection was lodged by an official body to the controversial planning permission.

# HOTEL LEAVES IN ITS WAKE DISMAY, SHOCK AND OPPOSITION

The hotel development, which is expected to be completed by mid 2006, has been greeted with shock and horror by organisations and individuals who are active in preserving Ireland's unique architectural and archaeological heritage.

Anngret Simms Professor of Historical Geography at University College Dublin said the hotel development significantly diminished the historical ambience of Trim Castle and its environs.

"The architecture of the hotel is completely out of tune with the scale of the medieval town. Because of its intrusive character in the immediate neighbourhood of one of the country's most important national monuments permission to build a hotel should not have been given on that site," Professor Simms said.

Few of the elected representatives in County Meath with the exception of the councillors who objected to selling the land to Mr O'Brien and Councillor Cantwell who tried to object to An Bord Pleanála have spoken out in opposition to the development.

The officials of the OPW and Dúchas who did so much to preserve and restore the monument, have spoken privately of their absolute outrage at what they consider to be the crass defacement of Trim Castle while international organisations like Europa Nostra, which awarded the Castle a heritage award in 2002, and many of the thousands of tourists who visit the castle where the film *Braveheart* was made a decade ago have also expressed their horror.

Set of *Braveheart* in Trim Castle.

the defacement of a
medieval national monument

# TRIM CASTLE

**The Minister and local authority are charged to protect our heritage. Do we now have to protect that heritage from them?**

A visitor entering the town of Trim in county Meath from the Dublin Road comes across one of Ireland's most imposing and impressive national monuments. With the view from its recently restored Keep to the Cooley mountains in the north east, the Dublin mountains to the south and across several counties to the west and north, the Norman built 12th century Trim Castle is recognised as one of the most significant surviving castles in Europe.

## A HISTORIC NATIONAL MONUMENT

Built over a period of seventy years from 1175 by Hugh de Lacy, the English baron appointed by Henry II, King of England as Justiciar of Ireland, and later by his son Walter, the castle dominates the medieval town of Trim and the surrounding landscape which is dotted with outlying churches, castles, gateways and other structures dating from the Norman settlement.

Strategically located, the castle provided substantial protection for the baron and the inhabitants of the medieval town which grew around its exterior along the banks of the river Boyne, against the threat from the Irish rebel chieftains to the north and west and from Strongbow to the south who was perceived as a potential challenger to the King of England. Through the centuries the castle's walls and gateways deteriorated and the surrounding moat was filled but the fundamental structures and stonework survived.

## IN 2004 A NEW THREAT TO THE CASTLE EMERGES

While the outlying lands to the east and south have been largely protected from development recent years have seen a dramatic encroachment within yards of the castle walls and within the environs of the national monument following a decision by the local authority, Trim Urban District Council (UDC), to allow the construction of a four storey hotel and car park in its shadow.

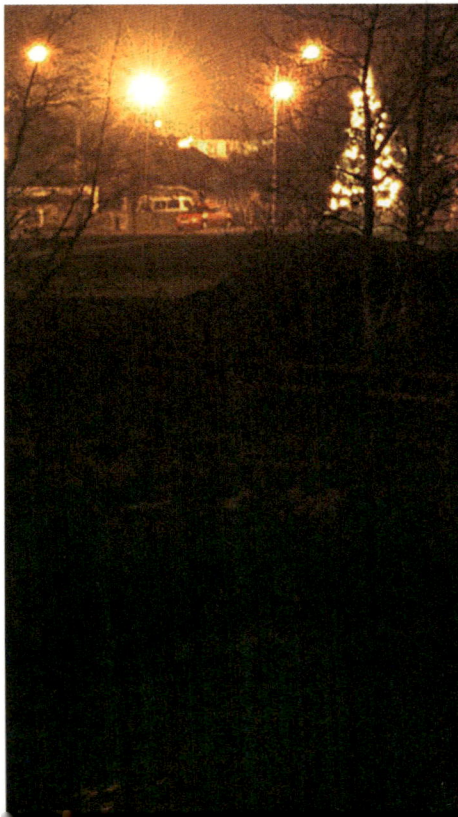

# Land deals, nuns' graves, brave hearts and bad faith

## THE STORY BEGINS

Purchased by the State from Lord Dunsany in 1993, Trim Castle was painstakingly restored to much of its former glory by dedicated professional staff from the Office of Public Works. Later it came under the control of Dúchas – the Heritage Service. The restoration of the Castle and its historic Keep and gatehouses was recommended in a 1994 report on the future of the national monument commissioned by the OPW from Arthur Gibney and Partners, the prominent Dublin firm of architects.

The restoration cost €4.46 million of which £3 million (€3.8 million) was provided under the EU funded operational programme for tourism 1994-99. In his report Arthur Gibney also recommended the provision of new car parking areas for visiting tourists, a requirement which became even more pressing following the 1995 filming in Trim Castle of *Braveheart* the story of the Scottish chieftain, William Wallace, featuring the Australian actor, Mel Gibson.

*Braveheart* set.

# The report was adopted by the Town Council and specifically emphasised the importance of the Castle and the need for any new development to respect this and other landmarks.

## COMMITTEES, CAR PARKS & COUNCIL PLANS

A liaison committee chaired by former Meath County manager Frank O'Brien was formed and included representatives of the Meath Heritage Centre, the chamber of commerce and county engineer, Oliver Perkins, who was later to become manager of Trim UDC or Trim Town Council, as it became known in January 2002.

In 1996 Meath County Council and Trim Town Council commissioned environmental consultants, Brady Shipman Martin, to prepare a master plan identifying proposals for further expansion of the town centre. The report was adopted by the Town Council and specifically emphasised the importance of the Castle and the need for any new development to respect this and other landmarks.

"The setting of the Castle, the river and the views to the town especially from the eastern approaches is critical to the character of the town. So too are the mature trees, the spire, towers and column which punctuate the horizon. New developments must respect these inimitable landmarks," the report concluded.

Discussions began for the assembly of land in order to satisfy the requirement of the Brady Shipman Martin report for additional car parking to facilitate the growing needs of Trims' almost 5,000 residents and of visitors to the heritage town.

Oliver Perkins, Manager of Trim Town Council

## THE OFFICE OF PUBLIC WORKS

The Office of Public Works (OPW) is a government department under the control of the Minister for Finance. The OPW is headed by a minister of state – currently Tom Parlon.

His predecessor from 1997 until 2002 was Martin Cullen who became Minister for the Environment in 2002 until he was moved to the Department of Transport in the cabinet reshuffle of September 2004.

In 1994 the newly formed Department of Arts, Culture and the Gaeltacht took over heritage policy. In 1996 Dúchas was established as the heritage section of the department.

In 1997 the department, under its then minister, Síle De Valera, was renamed the Department of Arts, Heritage, Gaeltacht and the Islands.

Following the general election of 2002 the Taoiseach, Bertie Ahern, announced the break up of Dúchas with responsibility for heritage policy being passed to the Department of the Environment under its new minister Martin Cullen with the exception of responsibility for national monuments which was transferred to the OPW.

However the OPW did not assume this responsibility until June 2004.

# THE LAND DEAL WITH THE NUNS

Mr Perkins played a central role in negotiating the purchase of land from the Sisters of Mercy for use as a car park to accommodate the expected increase in visitors to the Castle. The Mercy order had long held possession of the land, known as the Nun's Garden, through the charitable St Finian's Trust and was required to get permission from the Commissioners of Charitable Donations and Bequests to sell the land to the Town Council.

Permission was granted to the Sisters of Mercy to sell approximately 1.3 acres of land for the sum of £42,500 (€53,963) to the council. In 1997 the OPW agreed to provide £50,000 (€63,486) to the local authority to purchase and develop the land for a public car park.

According to Hugh Cumisky with Balbriggan based Cumisky Real Estate Alliance who acted as auctioneer for the nuns the order had understood from Meath County Council that their land was acquired for a public car park.

Eleven of their deceased members were exhumed in 1994 and their remains were moved from individual plots in the nuns garden to a common grave outside the town.

"During the course of my negotiations back in 1996 it was intimated to me that the site was being acquired for car parking purposes. I am not suggesting that was not the case at that time nor have I any evidence to suggest otherwise. Accordingly, it was with the benefit of hindsight some nine years later, when the site is being developed as a hotel, I am inclined to take a jaundiced view of the matter," said Mr Cumisky in reference to the fact that the nuns sold land now worth several million euro for the paltry sum of £42,500.

In January 1998, the Minister for Arts Heritage, Gaeltacht and the Islands, Síle de Valera, wrote to then Environment minister and local TD, Noel Dempsey, to confirm that an amount of £3.0 million had been allocated from EU funds to the Trim Castle project including a sum of £0.05m (£50,000) for car/bus parking.

Ms de Valera wrote: "As you know, an amount of £3.0 million has been allocated to the project from the EU Operational Programme for Tourism, 1994-1999 and it is envisaged that it will be spent as follows:

| | |
|---|---|
| Works to the Keep | £1.00m |
| Archaeology | £0.70m |
| Site Conservation Works | £0.50m |
| Site Facilities (toilets etc) | £0.30m |
| Car/bus parking | £0.05m |
| Interpretative material | £0.35m |
| Sundry | £0.10m |
| Total | £3.00m." |

In 2004, the Department of the Environment sought the repayment of the £50,000 of public monies given to the Town Council when it emerged that the car park had been passed into private hands.

# ...she was told that she would not obtain planning permission for a commercial development so close to the castle and that the council would impose a compulsory purchase order on the land if she did not agree to sell.

## THE COFFEE SHOP WHICH WAS A GREATER DEVELOPMENT THREAT THAN THE 4-STOREY HOTEL

In a further unusual transaction the local authority acquired a bungalow close to the roadway and the castle wall in order to facilitate access to the nuns land it had purchased for the car park. Negotiations took place with the owner John Davy who declined to sell the site to the council. Instead he passed it over to Sheila Kealey who looked after the late Mr Davy and his brothers for many years. When Ms Kealey said that she was interested in opening a guesthouse/coffee shop to service visitors to the castle she was told that she would not obtain planning permission for a commercial development so close to the castle and that the council were likely to impose a compulsory purchase order on the land if she did not agree to sell. She subsequently sold the land, which she was told was required for the planned car park, for £185,000 (€234,901) to the council.

"I feel devastated, sick and disgusted that there is now a hotel being built on the site when I was told there could be no commercial development there. I feel so hard done by, seeing what other people have gained," she said.

A shed, owned by a local doctor and also adjacent to her bungalow, was also purchased and knocked by the council to provide further access to the car park site.

## HOTEL DEVELOPMENT RULED OUT BY EXPERT REPORT

In 2001, Hassett Ducatez Architects were commissioned to recommend the best future use of the combined sites in the possession of the Town Council. The architects stated that a large or medium scale hotel would not be sustainable as "the large service yard and parking areas required may not be an ideal town centre pattern on this sensitive site." However, the report suggested that the site could be used for the development of hostel type accommodation.

## THE TENDERING PROCESS

On April 14, 2001 the manager of Trim Town Council, Oliver Perkins, who also retained the role of county engineer placed an advertisement with the local newspaper, the Meath Chronicle, inviting "expressions of interest in development opportunities at Castle Street" where the car park site had been assembled from the nuns, Ms Kealey and the local doctor, George Doyle. The advertisement stated that any proposals must be "in accordance with recommendations provided for in the Brady Shipman Martin Plan and Trim Urban Framework Plan adopted by Trim Urban District Council." In the invitations sent to prospective bidders the council said that "a specialist Advisory Panel set up for the purpose of assessment, shall advise the local authority. The local authority shall in its absolute discretion, be the sole judge of submissions and shall choose the successful submissions."

It stated that the proposal would be for an area of land comprising 0.4110 hectares within a block bounded by Castle Street and Castle Street car park.

## THE POWERFUL 'ADVISORY' COMMITTEE IS FORMED

In June 2001 a bidders conference took place where various developers were informed that a specialist advisory panel would be established to advise the local authority. The local authority, it said, shall "in its absolute discretion be the sole judge of submissions and shall choose the successful submission."

The panel of advisors was established and comprised of Mr Perkins, Dermot Mulligan of architects, Newenham Mulligan and Associates, Jimmy Farrelly, former secretary general of the Department of the Environment and Joe Crockett the assistant county manager for County Meath. By December 2001 the advisory committee had recommended the proposal for a 68 bedroom hotel with function rooms, leisure facilities and car park submitted by local developer David O'Brien. Another proposal by local builder Tom Hora, for a hostel and theatre with shops and other facilities was rejected although it conformed more closely to the recommendations in the report commissioned by the council from Hassett Ducatez.

Mr Hora has told the Centre for Public Inquiry that if competing developers had known that a hotel development was an acceptable option they would have submitted a proposal for such a project.

...a specialist advisory panel would be established to advise the local authority which shall "in its absolute discretion be the sole judge of submissions and shall choose the successful submission".

## DEVELOPER IS INFORMED BEFORE LOCAL AUTHORITY ELECTED MEMBERS

Within a day of the recommendation by the advisory panel Mr O'Brien was informed by letter that he had won the tender weeks before the elected councillors, who had agreed the formation of the advisory panel, were told. Indeed, a number of councillors complained that they had not been informed either of the purchase of the nuns land for a car park and were kept largely in the dark about developments in this key part of the town.

## LAND ACQUIRED FOR 'ROAD DEVELOPMENT'

As recommended by the advisory panel D. O'Brien Developments Ltd. proceeded to acquire an adjoining site to Ms Kealeys owned by Paul Gilroy to complete the assembly of the land for the hotel. Mr Gilroy has confirmed that he was paid over £400,000 for the site. Mr Gilroy also obtained planning permission to build a new house in Rathmolyon outside the town. In a letter from Aidan Collins executive planner with Meath County Council to Mr Perkins in January 2003 it was stated that the permission to Mr Gilroy for the new house should be granted as the purchase of his site opposite the castle walls was needed for a new "road development".

"There is an element of planning gain achieved in this application as the applicants current property is to be compulsorily acquired as part of a road development scheme within Trim," the memo from Mr Collins to Mr Perkins stated. In fact, the hotel is currently being constructed on the land formerly owned by Mr Gilroy and Ms Kealey as well as on that previously owned by the nuns.

## ADVISORS OR DECISION-MAKERS

In January 2002 the monthly meeting of Trim Town Council was informed by the manager, Mr Perkins, that the tender process had been completed. In his reply to a question from Councillor Danny O'Brien he described the four person group which recommended the hotel development as ' an independent adjudication panel" in contrast to its previous designation as an advisory panel. The terms "advisory panel" and "adjudication panel" are used at different times and in different documents and minutes over a period of several months.

According to the minutes of the meeting on January 8, 2002;

"The manager (Oliver Perkins) informed the members of the process to date, which concluded with assessment of the tenders, as previously agreed with members by an independent adjudication panel of Thursday 19th December 2001. The tenderer with the preferred proposal has been notified and asked to enter into pre-planning discussions with the planning authority to ensure that the proposal is acceptable. It is intended then to take the proposals to the Town and Area council members before formal disposal of the property can be initiated."

A discussion followed during which Cllrs O'Brien and Phillip Cantwell aired their concerns at the process.

"Councillor O'Brien indicated his complete disappointment with the procedure suggesting that the council was not being kept informed of the process. Management refuted this. Cllr O'Brien indicated his disappointment at the selection result and suggested that a meeting be held to receive details of how only two tenders were assessed from an original five and how the decision was finally reached."

"The manager reiterated that the members had given approval to respect the decision of an independent board and those proposals would be presented to the members after pre-planning discussions had been initiated."

Councillor Vincent McHugh concurred with the managers view that agreement was given that an independent adjudication board be appointed.

The minutes continued; "A lengthy and heated discussion ensued during which Cllr O'Brien suggested that public personnel did things improperly at various times. The Manager indicated that he found such comments offensive and advised the members of their duty to have issues investigated at the highest level if there was any feeling of inappropriate actions having been undertaken by public officials."

# COUNCILLORS RECALL WARNINGS OF LITIGATION

The former chairman of Trim Town Council, Peter Crinion, and elected council members including Jimmy Peppard, who voted in favour of the disposal and Phillip Cantwell who voted against, have told the Centre for Public Inquiry that they were informed by town manager, Oliver Perkins, that the council could face legal action if they did not accept the recommendation of an advisory panel to support the sale of council land to the developer.

According to Phillip Cantwell, an independent councillor who has been most vocal in his opposition to the hotel development, and who attributes the large vote he received in the 2002 local elections to his campaign against it, the former town manager argued that the recommendation of the advisory panel should be accepted by the members.

"We argued that the advisory panel was just that. Its job was to advise the elected councillors who would then make a decision. It was not a decision making panel as Mr Perkins argued," said Councillor Cantwell.

Former councillor, Chris Cleary (Fianna Fáil) agreed that the members were told that a failure to dispose of the land to Mr O'Brien could have "serious consequences for the council".

Mr Cleary said that he was in favour of the proposals for Trim set out in the Brady Shipman Martin report which did not include a hotel development close to the Castle walls.

Councillor Danny O'Brien (Independent Labour) was the only elected politician to object to the application for planning permission subsequently lodged by D. O'Brien Development Ltd. After meeting with developer, David O'Brien, who gave him assurances in relation to the scale of the development, Cllr Danny O'Brien decided not to appeal to An Bord Pleanála after the Trim Town Council granted planning permission.

"The council members were not kept fully informed and I believe we were duped into disposing of the site. We were told that if we didn't go along with the decision of the advisory panel we would be leaving ourselves open to litigation. I put in an objection to the planning application but I did not go to An Bord Pleanála. I spoke to (developer) David O'Brien and he talked to me about the scale of the development. One of the interesting things he told me is that the planners told him that the hotel had to be along the line of the old dwellings on the street. He was told to build very close to the road (and the castle walls). I would have preferred the other development proposed by builder, Tom Hora. I felt isolated at the time and did not see any great feeling among the people of Trim against the hotel," Councillor O'Brien said.

Councillor Gerry Reilly (FG) who is related through marriage to David O'Brien abstained on the vote for disposal of the land.

"The independent panel chose David O'Brien's development and we were unhappy that they did not come back (to the council). I have no problem with the hotel being so close to the Castle and have seen similar developments in other heritage towns."

Councillor Jimmy Peppard (Ind Labour) said that he only voted in favour of the disposal to Mr O'Brien to avoid the possible threat of litigation.

"In my view the hotel development is a huge blight on a heritage town. It does not fit with what councillors wanted there. The whole thing is shrouded and it should be teased out as to what happened. The hotel got planning despite the town development plan and the area action plan. There was supposed to be a two storey building there not a four storey one. The whole thing merits an inquiry. The manager asked permission to set up a panel but the final arbiters were the elected representatives. When the decision of the panel came back the manager said that if we did not comply we could be liable to a legal claim."

Councillor Peppard said that councillors were heavily dependant on the advice of planners and the manager who had many years experience as county engineer as well as Trim town manager.

He said that other developers in the area were not informed that a hotel would be acceptable on the site and if they had would have submitted plans for such a development. Tom Hora, the builder who submitted the unsuccessful tender – a hostel type development with a theatre – confirmed that he and others would have submitted proposals for a hotel if they had known it would have met with a favourable response from council officials.

Councillor Vincent McHugh said that he supports the hotel development which he claims will benefit the town and which has gone through "all the rigours of the law and planning procedures."

He claims that the councillors had agreed to hand the decision to the Advisory panel.

"I think we have to provide for the people of this century and we try to protect what was there two thousand years ago but there has to be a happy medium," he said.

The chairman of Meath County Council Brian Fitzgerald (Ind) said that county councillors had no role in the hotel development although he personally was unhappy with the nature and scale of the development so close to the Castle walls.

"I would prefer to see a different type of building and I would prefer to see it set back further from the hotel," said Councillor Brian Fitzgerald.

Centre for Public Inquiry

The same view with the hotel development, September 2005

## THE DEBATE RAGES ON

At a subsequent meeting on February 12, 2002 the debate continued to rage with the manager promising that the preferred proposal of the adjudication panel would be the subject of pre-planning discussions in advance of the signing of a legal contract. He also indicated that the notice of the formal disposal of council property to the developer would issue to the members for their approval. Chairman of the council, Peter Crinion, suggested that "the matter was taken out of the hands of the council by informing the successful tenderer before the council met thereby removing the council's reserved function/right in relation to the proposed disposal."

On March 4, 2002 Meath County Council adopted the Trim Development Plan which included in its recommendations that the view from St Patrick's Church to Trim Castle be preserved. The specific recommendation adopted by councillors is contained in Section 4.11 of the plan under the heading *Views and Prospects*.

In May 2002, the councillors were provided with the notice for the disposal of the lands at Castle Street. At a town council meeting on May 14th a row ensued with Cllr O'Brien claiming that the final decision on the development was with the councillors and not with the independent adjudication panel as it was now being described in the council minutes. According to Cllr Cantwell only the elected members could agree to the disposal of land.

The minutes record; "Councillor Cantwell suggested that while the proposal for Castle Street was of major significance for the town he did not consider it the most suitable for this location. Cllr O'Brien expressed concern and queried if the council had in fact the final decision on the proposal. The Manager reiterated the process to date and stated that this formal disposal was the climax of prescribed procurement procedure. In response, Cllr O'Brien suggested that while the independent adjudication panel had been given power by this council to make a judgement on their behalf the final decision should rest with the elected members."

Councillor Cantwell suggested that while the proposal for Castle Street was of major significance for the town he did not consider it the most suitable for this location. Cllr O'Brien expressed concern and queried if the Council had in fact the final decision on the proposal.

When the planning application arrived for a hotel within the curtilage of the historic Trim Castle alarm bells immediately rang within the department and particularly among those officials responsible for archaeology, architecture and the environment.

Cllr Cleary said that the proposal did not conform to the Brady Shipman Martin report and suggested postponing the disposal decision until the members got legal advice. Cllr Cantwell also proposed to suspend the disposal pending the council seeking legal advice but got no seconder for his motion, according to the minutes of the May meeting.

## COUNCILLORS AGREE TO DISPOSE OF LANDS

The minutes indicate that Councillors Crinion and McHugh suggested that the disposal of the property to Mr O'Brien, as recommended by the adjudication panel, should proceed although Mr Crinion now claims that this minute does not reflect his views. Mr Perkins insists that he exercised no influence on the members to dispose of the lands.

"The councillors had the reserve function to sanction the disposal of property. All I would have said is that they would have to explain why they did not accept the advice of an independent panel. I've never known where a manager did not accept the recommendations of an advisory panel," Mr Perkins told the Centre for Public Inquiry.

Cllr McHugh proposed to go ahead with the disposal of the property and the motion was seconded by Cllr Griffith. The two councillors were supported by Cllrs Crinion, Lenihan, Peppard and O'Brien with Cllrs Cantwell and Cleary against. Cllr Reilly, a relation through marriage of the developer, abstained.

## LAND ACQUIRED AND PLANNING APPLICATION LODGED

Following further discussions with the planners David O'Brien acquired 3465.87 sq metres of land for £253,950 (€322,449) and road works to the value of £314,895 (€399,834) for the purposes of building a four star hotel, car parking and other facilities. Meath County Council at this time also disposed of the Kealey land of approximately 717.86 sq metres to Mr O'Brien giving him a total of approximately 4183.73 sq metres of council owned property.

Several months later a planning application for a hotel comprising 68 bedrooms was submitted to the Town Council on February 21, 2003.

## THE ROLE OF THE MINISTER AND HIS DEPARTMENT

The Department of the Environment was duly informed of the planning application in its role as statutory consultees in the planning process. A year previously the remit for Dúchas – the Heritage Service was moved to the Department of the Environment. When the planning application arrived for a hotel within the curtilage of the historic Trim Castle alarm bells immediately rang within the department and particularly among those officials responsible for archaeology, architecture and the environment.

Dúchas made several observations/submissions in relation to the development to the Minister for Environment, Martin Cullen, who had been appointed to a full cabinet position in June 2002 following a period as junior minister with responsibility for the OPW in the previous Fianna Fáil-Progressive Democrat administration.

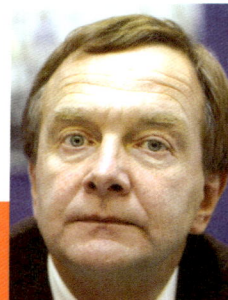

Martin Cullen, the then Minister for Environment

## THE MINISTER VERSUS HIS HERITAGE OFFICIALS

An intriguing exchange of correspondence took place between the heritage officials and the minister whose policy co-ordinator Fearga O'Coigligh was given responsibility for what was clearly perceived as a delicate matter. The minister and the Taoiseach, Bertie Ahern, were already under some criticism over the break up of Dúchas and were accused of weakening the heritage protection agencies. Dúchas personnel were concerned, with some justification, that the heritage service was being downgraded to facilitate roads and other infrastructure. Environmentalists complained that the minister was wearing contradictory hats with responsibility to protect the environment on the one hand while clearly encouraging projects within government that threatened the natural and built environment.

The threat to Trim Castle by the commercial development in its shadow was seen as a litmus test of the government's commitment to Ireland's heritage and whether it was prepared to sacrifice the integrity of a national monument to short term commercial interests.

According to Dúchas officials, who communicated their concerns to the local authorities Meath County Council and Trim Town Council, the proposed hotel was "more appropriate to a dense urban context rather than to a country town" and that the development had the "potential to impact not only on the National Monument but also on a number of protected structures on Castle Street." The officials also informed the minister through his policy co-ordinator of their deep concerns.

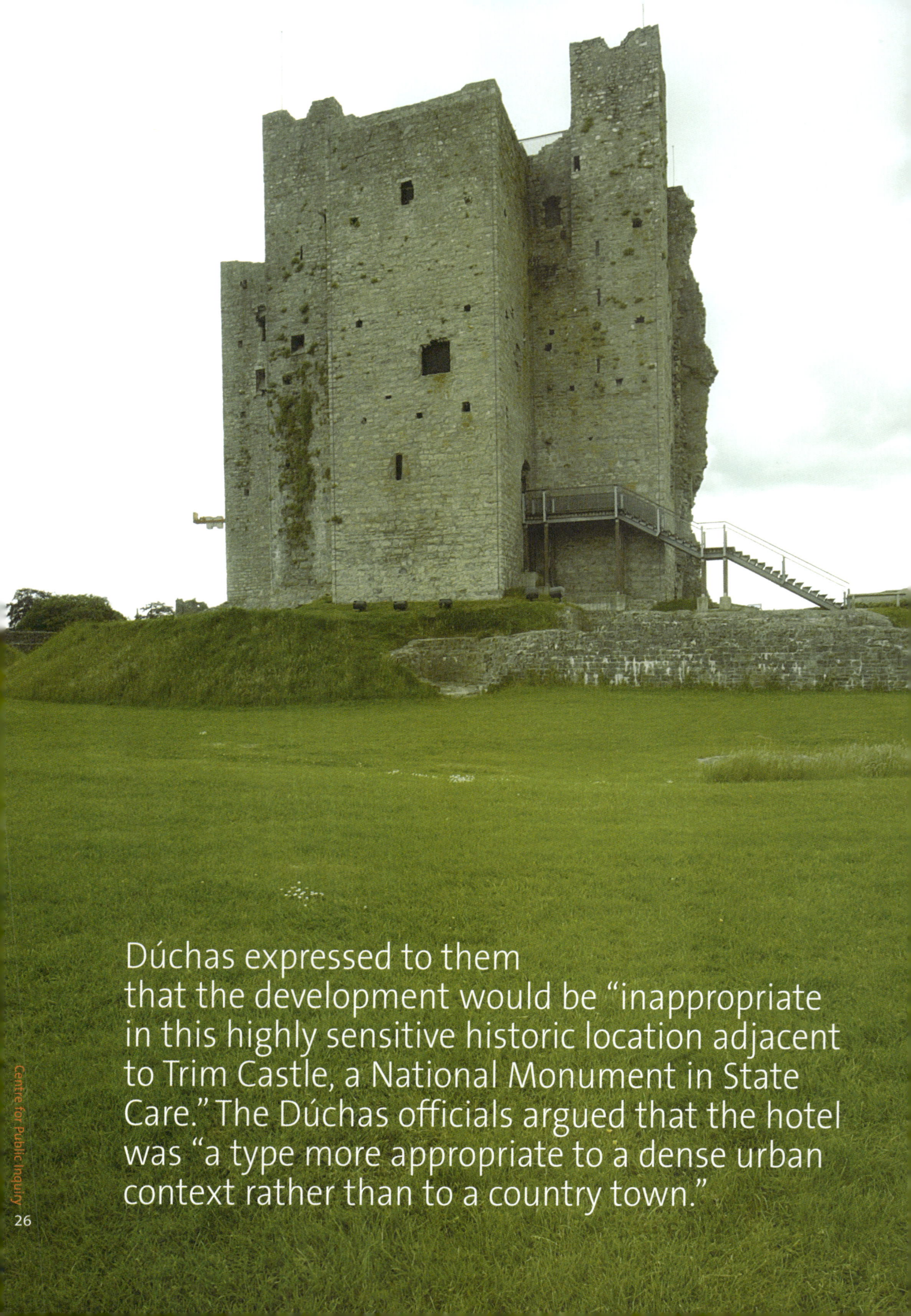

Dúchas expressed to them
that the development would be "inappropriate
in this highly sensitive historic location adjacent
to Trim Castle, a National Monument in State
Care." The Dúchas officials argued that the hotel
was "a type more appropriate to a dense urban
context rather than to a country town."

## MINISTER IGNORES EXPERT ADVICE

Documents sought under the FOI and released to the Centre for Public Inquiry have revealed that the former minister, Martin Cullen, ignored repeated recommendations by his officials to oppose the development of the hotel opposite Trim Castle, which they described as a national monument in state care.

Dúchas officials had met with Mr O'Brien's development team, led by architects Christopher Flynn and Associates on May 15, 2003 to discuss alternative ways in which the visual impact on the hotel could be reduced. The officials proposed that the development be spread over more of the site to reduce the impact, reduce the number of bedrooms and reduce the internal spaces. Since the development team were not eager to take on board these proposals, Dúchas agreed to look at revisions designed to reduce the impact by pulling back the upper floors.

Robert O'Grady from Dúchas wrote to Christopher Flynn & Associates who represented the developer on June 10, 2003 after some revisions were submitted to the Town Council and passed on to the department. In his letter, he refers to the meeting that took place on May 15, 2003 when Dúchas expressed to them that the development would be "inappropriate in this highly sensitive historic location adjacent to Trim Castle, a National Monument in State Care". The Dúchas officials argued that the hotel was "a type more appropriate to a dense urban context rather than to a country town" and the hotel had "the potential to impact not only on the National Monument but also on a number of protected structures on Castle Street."

Mr O'Grady told the architects, in his letter of June 10, that "while part of the upper floors have been pulled back, a four-storey high corner element remains and has been altered to include less glazing than before..." and "it would appear that this corner section is higher than the medieval curtain of Trim Castle." Therefore "it is clear that this development would have an adverse and unacceptable effect on the setting and.... we continue to have concerns regarding the proposed development."

## THE EUROPA NOSTRA AWARD

Mr. O'Grady also pointed out in his letter that the castle had recently received a major international award and the citation for the Europa Nostra Diploma. Europa Nostra is an EU recognised preservation body which protects historic monuments.

"The restoration project has provided a better understanding of the early Norman settlement of Ireland, a pivotal moment in Irish and European history," the citation reads.

# "...the construction of a hotel on the site of a public car park may create pressure to provide additional public parking for cars and coaches adjacent to the castle, which in our opinion would be inappropriate."

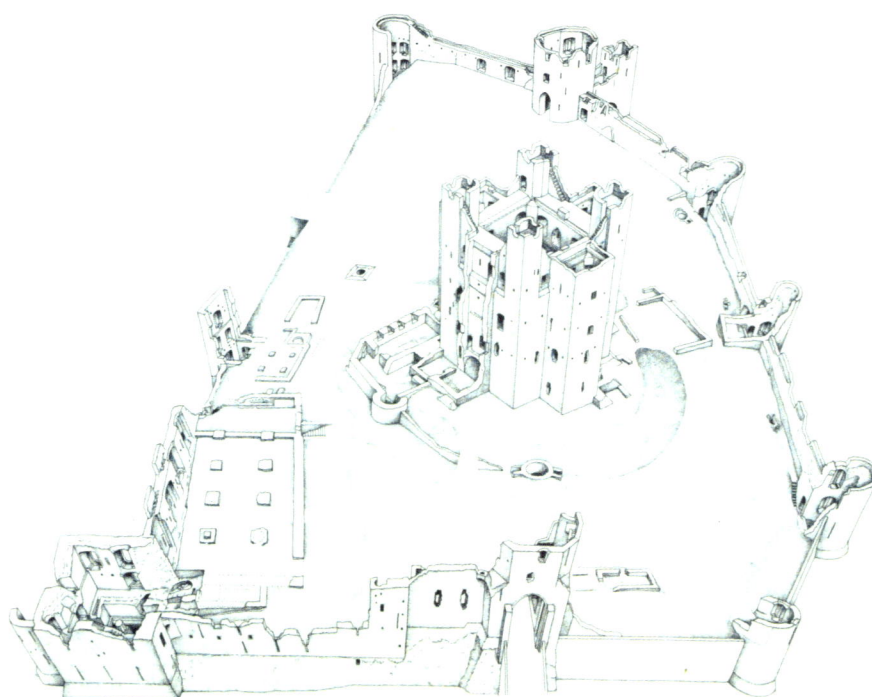

## HERITAGE EXPERTS CONTINUED TO PRESS THEIR CASE

Dúchas was clearly keen to ensure that no development would take away from the castle's significant importance as a national monument.

On June 26, 2003 Christopher Flynn & Associates sent what were described as "final revisions and drawings" to Trim Town Council which reduced the number of bedrooms from 68 to 63.

These latest alterations, however, did not satisfy the Dúchas officials.

On July 29, 2003 the developer and his architects agreed to further scale back the development and reduced the number of bedrooms from 63 to 58.

The hotel development went on a list of cases for Ministerial Approval on July 24, 2003. Dúchas officials outlined to the minister their opinion that the scale of the hotel would be appropriate in a dense urban context rather than a country town and that it had the potential to impact on other protected structures on Castle Street. Furthermore they pointed out that the officials were concerned "that the construction of an hotel on the site of a public car park may create pressure to provide additional public parking for cars and coaches adjacent to the castle, which in our opinion would be inappropriate."

"this development, due to its scale and bulk would have an adverse and negative impact on the setting and visual appreciation of Trim Castle and a number of protected structures. Consequently we recommend that the Planning Authority refuse permission for the development as currently proposed."

## DEVELOPMENT A THREAT TO THE LARGEST MEDIEVAL CASTLE IN IRELAND

The Dúchas officials said that they had requested further information "as we were concerned that the bulk and scale of the proposed development may have a negative visual impact on the setting and appreciation of the impressive Trim Castle, the largest medieval castle in Ireland which is also of international significance. At present, the Castle and area enclosed by the curtain wall dominates the approach to Trim Town and it was considered that a development on this scale could detract from its unique setting."

Archaeologists in the department were also concerned that significant material of historic interest would be lost unless further testing was carried out in the car park and link road area around the proposed hotel.

Dúchas officials advised the minister that they had "consistently expressed concern regarding the scale and bulk of the proposed development which we believe to be inappropriate in this highly sensitive historic location adjacent to Trim Castle, a National Monument in state care". In their recommendations, Dúchas officials pointed out that they had met with the development team and had agreed to look at revisions designed to reduce the impact of the development on the castle by pulling back the upper floors. However they pointed out that "despite these revisions and subsequent ones, it continues to be our opinion that this development, due to its scale and bulk would have an adverse and negative impact on the setting and visual appreciation of Trim Castle and a number of protected structures. Consequently we recommend that the Planning Authority refuse permission for the development as currently proposed."

Feargal O'Coigligh, the policy co-ordinator acting on behalf of Mr Cullen, responded six days later on July 30, 2003, to Treasa Langford in the Development Applications Section of the department rejecting the vigorous efforts of the heritage officials to block the hotel development. Mr O'Coigligh wrote:

# "A well designed modern building in the vicinity of the medieval building can have the potential to offer a contrasting and enhancing counterpoint to the existing built heritage," Mr O'Coigligh stated.

"It is considered that the department should not recommend refusal of this development, however, it should be recommended that the bulk and scale of the front façade be scaled/stepped back in order not to dominate the appreciation of the castle...A well designed modern building in the vicinity of the medieval building can have the potential to offer a contrasting and enhancing counterpoint to the existing built heritage," Mr O'Coigligh stated. He described the visitor centre situated within the walls of King John's Castle in Limerick as an example of how such a modern structure could complement an historic monument. He said that the developers and the local authority should ensure that the development will not cause car parking pressures in a manner that would adversely affect the castle.

On August 5, 2003, Trim Town Council sent a letter to Dúchas to inform them that further information had been obtained from the developer and was available for inspection. Dúchas had until the 15 August to look at the information obtained and to make a submission.

In an e-mail to Liam O'Connell Principal Officer with Dúchas, on August 6, Mr O'Coigligh restated his preference for a scaling back of the development.

"The option is to seek scaling back as part of the planning decision or to seek refusal. It is considered that the request to scale back be the appropriate response from the department," he wrote.

He asked Mr O'Connell to keep him posted on discussions that take place between the developer, Meath County Council and department officials.

# To be acceptable as a development at this location as one that would not irreversibly damage the unique value of the national monument and its environs, it is considered that a radical redesign involving a reduction in the scale of the development would be required.

## THE AMENDED LETTER

Treasa Langford sent to Mr O'Coigligh, for his approval, a copy of a draft letter she had written for Trim Town Council setting out the concerns of the heritage officials. It came back to her with significant amendments. Compared to the language and tone employed by Mr O'Coigligh in his alterations to the draft Ms Langford's letter was hard hitting and to the point.

Ms Langford wrote "To be acceptable as a development at this location as one that would not irreversibly damage the unique value of the national monument and its environs, it is considered that a radical redesign involving a reduction in the scale of the development would be required. The present proposal of a 400-seat function room together with associated facilities including shop, bar, gymnasium and almost 60 bedrooms on a restricted site has inevitably resulted in a building which is inappropriately large at this location. This still applies notwithstanding amendments already made to the proposals by the developer which, fall far short of, and have not resulted in the appropriate reduction in scale."

In conclusion "we strongly urge the Council, in its consideration of this development, to take account of the fact that such an inappropriate development in the vicinity of Trim Castle will detract from its unique setting and have a permanent, negative impact on the visual appreciation of one of Ireland's premier national monuments".

Ironically, Feargal O'Coigligh 'scaled back' her letter, omitting her paragraph about the developers revisions falling 'far short' of reducing the scale of the development. The sentence beginning with 'we strongly urge the Council', was toned down to read;

"Therefore in considering this application the planning authority should ensure that the development does not negatively impact on the visual appreciation of Trim Castle and other major elements of the built heritage in Trim, that it be scaled back where appropriate, particularly at the front of the proposed development, and that appropriate conditions are imposed in relation to the preservation of the archaeological heritage, by record or otherwise."

Before Ms Langford sent the revised letter to Trim Town Council she added pointedly that "this scaling back has not been achieved by the amendments already made to the proposal by the developers."

## Ironically, Feargal O'Coigligh 'scaled back' her letter, omitting her paragraph about the developers revisions falling 'far short' of reducing the scale of the development.

As a result of the instructions from the minister's office no objection was submitted by the Department or Dúchas officials to the planning application.

## PLANNING PERMISSION GRANTED DESPITE EXPERT CONCERNS

This letter was forwarded to Trim Town Council, but despite the concerns raised by Dúchas in this letter, the Council wrote to Dúchas on August 28, 2003 to inform them that planning permission had been granted for a 58 bedroom hotel subject to 28 conditions.

Dúchas had also expressed concern that an Archaeological Impact Assessment submitted with the planning application did not address the visual impact of the development on the Castle and did not address the impact the proposed link road from Castle Street towards Emmet Street and the proposed car park will have on archaeological heritage. The

Dúchas officials reiterated their view on numerous occasions that the "castle and area enclosed by the curtain wall dominates the approach to Trim town and it is considered that a development on this scale could detract from its unique setting."

As a result of the instructions from the minister's office no objection was submitted by the department or Dúchas officials to the planning application. Cllr Danny O'Brien objected to the planning permission but the Town Council proceeded to grant it on August 27, 2003. Following the granting of permission the chief archaeologist in the department, Brian Duffy, and his colleague Pauline Gleeson prepared an objection to the permission to An Bord Pleanála, the planning appeals board.

# In effect, an executive decision had been taken by the minister, Mr Cullen, to ignore the recommendations of Dúchas whose primary role was to protect Ireland's heritage.

## NATIONAL MONUMENTS SECTION BACKS UP HERITAGE OFFICIALS

In their letter of September 16 to the board seen by the Centre for Public Inquiry they stated; "that the National Monuments Section of this department concurs with the recommendations of the Architectural Heritage Advisory Section and consider that the development due to its scale and bulk will have a negative impact on the setting and visual appreciation of Trim Castle, a National Monument of international significance in State Ownership." They enclosed a cheque for €200, the cost of lodging an appeal.

Dave Fadden from the Heritage Section and Mr Duffy both believed that an appeal should be lodged on the grounds that the planning authority did not take on board their recommendations to ensure that the development would not have a negative impact on the castle. The heritage officials also re-inforced their views in correspondence with the minister's office.

"In summary, it is felt that this proposed development would have a significant adverse impact on the setting and amenity of Trim Castle a monument of the highest architectural, historical and archaeological significance. While some modifications to the original proposals have been made, these do not address the fundamental problem of the proposed development being over-large for such a site in an architecturally and historical sensitive location. Accordingly, it is recommended that the planning authority's decision to grant permission for the development be appealed to An Bord Pleanála," they wrote.

Mr O'Coigligh, however, claimed that the concerns of the heritage section had been addressed in the conditions and that "while concerns may still remain regarding the scale of the development as now

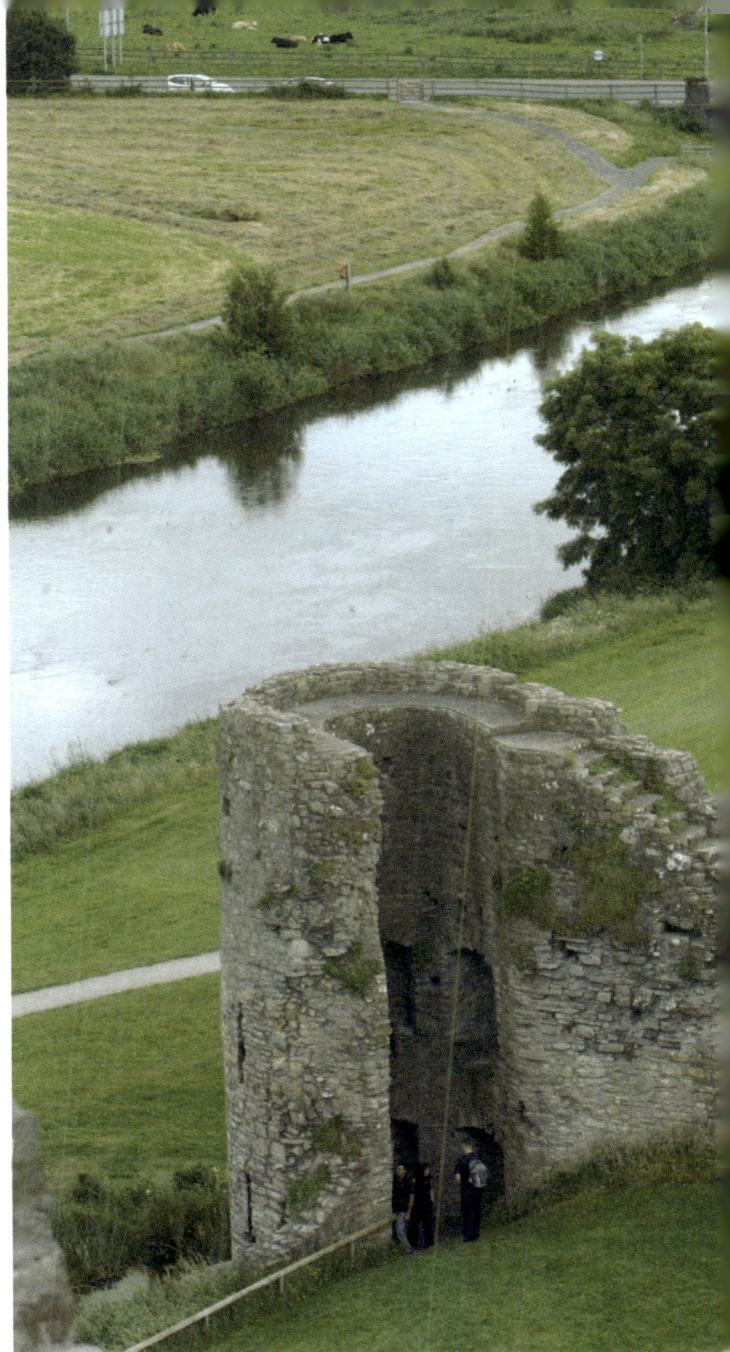

revised, it is considered that reasonable efforts have been made by the developer and Trim Town Council and an appeal to An Bord Pleanála by the department is not justified in this instance."

This intervention put a halt to the efforts by the most senior heritage officials to lodge an appeal to the board.

In effect, an executive decision had been taken by the minister, Mr Cullen, to ignore the recommendations of Dúchas whose primary role was to protect Ireland's heritage.

In a discussion on *Prime Time* in June 2004 with Dr Mark Clinton, an experienced archaeologist and chair of An Taisce's Monuments and Antiquities Committee, Mr Cullen defended the decision to ignore his own senior heritage officials and allow the hotel development to proceed.

Confirming his direct role in the controversial decision Mr Cullen said that he had asked his advisors what they thought would be a balanced approach. "They told me and I said, right go back to the county council involved and say that we would accept a much reduced proposal rather than the original, rather than going to An Bord Pleanála."

Asked by the Centre for Public Inquiry to comment on the fact that the hotel was now larger in terms of bedrooms and car parking spaces than the project he sought to have scaled back, a spokesman for Mr Cullen said: "The minister was advised by his heritage officials at the time and the role he would have played would have been on the back of that advice."

When it was pointed out that his heritage officials had attempted to stop the development and were not satisfied with the alterations made, the spokesman replied: "The issue was with the design. We didn't want the development as proposed. The minister said go back to the developer and if he fails to make the changes we will deal with the matter then. The developer agreed to make the changes."

When it was again pointed out that two of the most senior department officials, Brian Duffy and Dave Fadden, continued to object even after planning permission was granted and prepared a letter objecting to the permission for An Bord Pleanála on behalf of the department the spokesman said:

"The minister was responsible. The buck stops with the elected person. The original proposal raised issues from a heritage perspective. The minister decided to ask people to make the changes rather than go down the road (of objecting) that would take time and money."

Asked his opinion of the development now that An Bord Pleanála had given a recent decision to allow an increase in the number of bedrooms and car parking spaces, the spokesman said: "Take that up with the Department of the Environment. Mr Cullen is now the Minister for Transport."

The Minister for the Environment, Dick Roche, had no comment to make on the An Bord Pleanála decision.

## LOCAL EXPERT ON TRIM CASTLE LODGES AN OBJECTION

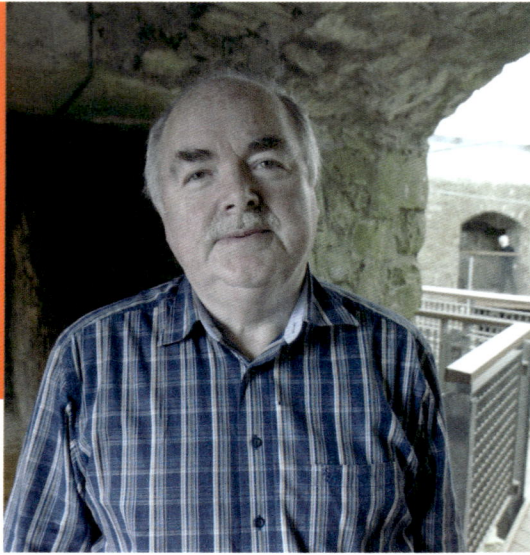

Cllr Phillip Cantwell, who opposed the development.

The only objection submitted to the appeals board was made by one of its own inspectors, Dermot Kelly, who has a keen academic interest in the national monuments in his native Trim and has written extensively on the Castle.

On September 22, 2003 he submitted an objection supported by UCD Professor of Historical Geography, Anngret Simms, and independent councillor Phillip Cantwell of Trim Town Council. The environmental organisation, An Taisce, also wrote a letter supporting the objection. In his objection Mr Kelly said that the proposed hotel development at the Castle Street entrance to the town would seriously contravene the resolutions of the International Council on Monuments and Sites (ICOMOS). He said that the Bruges Resolution on the Conservation of Smaller Historic Towns require states to "observe the existing scale of the town in all new developments, to respect its character, its dominant buildings and its relation to the landscape."

He stated that the overall scale of the development would contravene the Trim Town Development Plan 2002 which requires that "development in the vicinity of listed buildings will only be permitted where the characters and settings of such buildings are not considered impaired by the proposals."

Mr Kelly pointed out that two letters from Dúchas outlining these concerns were mislaid in the public file held in the offices of Trim Town Council.

Mr Kelly said that the proposed hotel development at the Castle Street entrance to the town would seriously contravene the resolutions of the International Council on Monuments and Sites (ICOMOS). He said that the Bruges Resolution on the Conservation of Smaller Historic Towns require states to "observe the existing scale of the town in all new developments, to respect its character, its dominant buildings and its relation to the landscape."

## AN TAISCE SUPPORTS MR KELLY'S OBJECTION

In supporting his objection An Taisce wrote that the development "would constitute a serious and irreversible negative intrusion on the character and setting of a monument of prime importance" and that the development would be "contrary to best conservation practice and the statutory guidelines for architectural heritage" as well as being "contrary to the provisions of current legislation for the proper protection for national monuments.'

The National Monuments Act specifically precludes the disturbance of soil or the excavation of the site of a monument without a licence. While a licence was issued to the developer to carry out an archaeological search the objectors have complained that significant material of archaeological interest may not have been recovered and preserved.

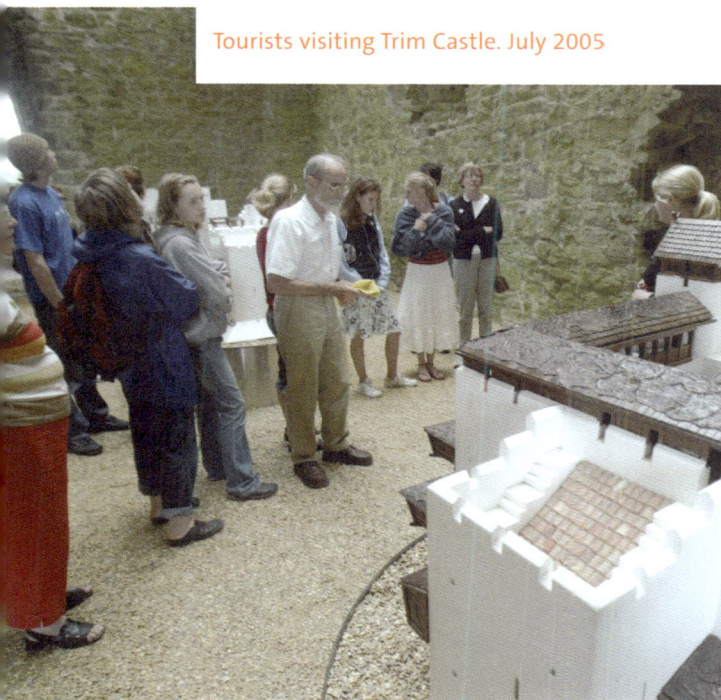

Tourists visiting Trim Castle. July 2005

## KELLY IS FORCED TO WITHDRAW OBJECTION

In response to Mr Kelly's objections Simon Clear a planning and development consultant acting for the developer David O'Brien wrote to An Bord Pleanála on October 22, 2003.

He claimed that as an inspector with An Bord Pleanála Mr Kelly had a potential conflict of interest in his objection to the planning permission. In his 27 page letter Mr Clear questioned how the impartiality and transparency of An Bord Pleanála could be ensured in relation to its handling of the appeal. He claimed the applicant, Mr Kelly had "adopted a singular mother-hen approach protective attitude based on the confined issue of heritage protection."

Following discussions with his superiors Mr Kelly withdrew his appeal explaining in a subsequent letter to An Bord Pleanála that he had made his decision "lest there be any possibility of any misconception or misconstruction by any party or any person that the appeal would not have been determined with absolute impartiality by An Bord Pleanála."

A request by the supporters of Mr Kelly's objection, Anngret Simms and Phillip Cantwell, to be allowed pursue the application was refused leaving the way clear for the construction of the hotel.

An Bord Pleanála granted permission to the developer to extend the hotel by increasing the number of bedrooms from 58 to 68 with an additional 54 car parking spaces.

In November 2004 D. O'Brien Developments Ltc. submitted a second planning application to Trim Town Council for an additional twelve bedrooms and 54 car parking spaces. Planning permission was granted in January 2005 but was appealed by An Taisce.

This appeal was rejected and on June 13, 2005 An Bord Pleanála granted permission to the developer to extend the hotel by increasing the number cf bedrooms from 58 to 68 with an additional 54 car parking spaces.

The hotel currently under construction, and due for completion by mid 2006, contains more bedrooms and car park spaces than envisaged thus undermining the publicly stated claims of the former minister, Mr Cullen, that his officials had achieved a "scaling back" of the development.

David O'Brien the developer of the 4 storey hotel in Trim told the Centre for Public Inquiry that he was happy with the design work on the hotel and said that the final construction would not obtrude on the historic Trim Castle.

"I put in an awful lot of work into the tender proposal, I got the best people to design it and I put a strong package in front of the panel," Mr O'Brien said.

In his opinion the hotel does not obstruct the views from the castle or the church grounds. Mr. O'Brien said that he was surprised that senior Dúchas officials wanted to prevent him getting planning permission for the hotel developmer t.

"I would be very surprised to hear that this was true. We were in negotiations with Dúchas. We knew that Dúchas would determine exactly what was going to be built here. We were prepared to do whatever Dúchas required."

He said that he did not think the hotel would have a negative impact on views from or to the Castle.

"I don't think it will have an impact on the castle. Dúchas asked us to set back the third and fourth floor. It was my understanding that they were then satisfied."

# "It is now clear that the Department have not accepted the case that we put forward for the retention of the grant and that I intend to make the refund..."

A member of the advisory or adjudication panel, Dermot Mulligan, from architects firm Newenham Mulligan & Associates, said that he was appointed by the county manager to the advisory committee.

He recalled that score sheets on the tenders were provided by Oliver Perkins and "we sat and talked about it and came to a joint decision."

Jimmy Farrelly, former secretary general of the Department of the Environment said that he believed that the role of the panel was as advisers to the elected members.

"I am operating from recollection. It would have been hard to say that it was an adjudication panel because it was subject to all statutory procedures. There was another factor involved with this as well. All or a substantial part of land involved had to be sold to a developer. This would have been a reserved function of the elected members and it would also be subject to the full planning process."

Joe Crockett, then assistant manager of County Meath was also on the panel. He recalled going through the submissions and there were arguments put forth for the proposals.

"I don't have a problem with the principle of a hotel on the site. I don't think that it has any impact on the castle," Mr. Crockett, who is now Carlow county manager, said.

"In medieval times there were always houses around the castle. It was the centre of economic power in the area," he said.

current town clerk of Trim Town Council, Larry tee, said that the hotel had gone through a us planning process.

of the hotel is that this whole process went

Jimmy Farrelly, former secretary general of the Department of Environment

through a planning process. It was there for the public to have their say to make their submissions. A decision was granted. The process that has been gone through has been fair and everything is above board and that is it as far as I am concerned."

## DEPARTMENT ASKS TOWN COUNCIL TO REPAY MONEY

Within the Department of the Environment and at the Dail Committee of Public Accounts (PAC) there was a growing disquiet about the allocation of £50,000 (€63,486) of public monies for the purchase of lands for a public car park which subsequently ended up in private hands. The Minister for the Environment, Dick Roche, who replaced Martin Cullen in the September 2004 cabinet reshuffle, sought the return of the money from Trim Town Council a move that was confirmed to the PAC in March 2005.

At a meeting of the Dail committee on March 24, 2005 the secretary general of the Department of the Environment, Niall Callan, said that the money had been "unequivocally promised" to the Department.

"The money has been unequivocally promised to

the Department. To the best of my knowledge it has not yet reached the Department's account but it is not an issue between ourselves and Meath County Council. We requested the money back and were promised a cheque. I am not sure whether the cheque has been lodged to our account," Mr Callan told the vice-chairman of the committee, John McGuinness (FF).

In late August, 2005, town manager Kevin Stewart wrote to the members of Trim Town Council to tell them that he intended to repay the £50,000 (€63,486).

"It is now clear that the Department have not accepted the case that we put forward for the retention of the grant and that I intend to make the refund in the next few days," he told councillors in a letter on August 24th.

He said that one of the reasons for the Department's

decision was that "a large sum of money was received for the sale of the site concerned."
At an emergency meeting on September 6th, called in response to his letter, five councillors led by Danny O'Brien (Ind) demanded that the payment be withheld until officials of the Department attended a council meeting to properly explain their reasons for demanding the refund. A motion to this effect was passed unanimously.

Mr. Stewart explained that he could not compel Department officials to meet the members. However he agreed to write to them inviting them to attend a meeting. His legal advice also confirmed that the decision to make the repayment was one for the manager and not the members.

"The decision as to whether or not to refund the money is an executive decision, which means that

# "This hotel development is crazy. It is far too near (the castle).
It goes against our principal idea.
That would have been a perfect place for a car park," – Gibney

it is down to me basically. That's the legal position. I have to make a decision based on what I believe are the long term interests of Trim Town Council and Trim town."

"I would not see any merit at any time in being off side with the Department.  In fairness we have a good relationship with them... and I would like to keep it that way."

Despite his comments some councillors continued to resist repaying the funds,  most recently in a motion drafted for a meeting of Trim Town Council on September 19th last.

## EU CONCERNS OVER PLANNING PROCESS

On foot of correspondence from Councillor Cantwell the EU's Environment Commissioner has also launched an investigation into the possible abuse of €3.8 million EU funds provided for the restoration of the Castle. The complaints procedure is focused on whether the local authority carried out an Environmental Impact Assessment or at least screened the planning application in order to establish whether an EIA was required under EU ᵗ'es. Officials from the complaints office have ⸱ten in recent months to the Irish government's ⸱anent representative in Brussels seeking ⸱s to a series of questions and in recent ⸱ave sought further clarifications to the

replies they have received from the Irish authorities. They have sought to establish whether Trim Town Council or any other relevant authority has maintained a written record of any deliberations by planning officials on an EIA process. Under EU legislation an EIA must be at least considered where a project threatens to damage the environment or historic monuments.

A senior EU official confirmed to the Centre for Public Inquiry in early September that it had acted on a complaint made by Councillor Cantwell to the Environment Commissioner in January 2005. Councillor Cantwell alleged that the local authority had not carried out an EIA prior to granting planning permission for the four storey hotel only metres from Trim Castle.

"We wrote to the Irish government asking them whether a screening decision had been taken and on what grounds the decision was made and whether that decision had been made public.  The Irish government responded but they haven't fully clarified their position. The government is due to meet with EU officials in October to discuss the issue of Trim Castle and other general environmental issues," the official said.

Another senior administrator in the Environment Commission, Liam Cashman, confirmed that the complaints procedure should be completed within a year of the original complaint and said that the details and results of the investigation would not be revealed until that time. Last year in a significant ruling the European Court of Justice ruled that proper records of the EIA process should be retained by local and national authorities

As well as departmental, Dail and EU concerns Arthur Gibney, the architect who prepared the original report on the best means of enhancing the area surrounding the castle, commissioned by the UDC in 1994, has also expressed his disappointment at the hotel development.

"This hotel development is crazy.  It is far too near the castle. It goes against our principal idea. That would have been a perfect place for a car park," Mr Gibney told the Centre for Public Inquiry.

# interview

"

**A**nngret Simms is a Professor of Historical Geography in the Department of Geography in UCD. She was joint editor of the Irish Historic Towns Atlas, published by the Royal Irish Academy and has considerable expertise in the topographical history of Irish towns. Dermot Kelly's objection was co-signed by Professor Simms who supported his concerns. When Kelly's objection was withdrawn, the Professor was informed by An Bord Pleanála that as a co-signatory her objection did not carry any weight and that her concerns would not be recognised as a stand alone objection to the hotel.

Professor Simms says that she is well aware of the problematic procedures that led to the purchase of the site by the builder of the hotel, but she believes that the hotel is in breach of the spirit of the National Monuments Act 1930 (as amended by the National Monuments (Amendment) Act 2004) and the Trim Town Development Plan 2002.

According to Professor Simms, "a large four-storey hotel directly opposite Trim Castle will significantly diminish the historical ambience of the place. The hotel is grossly over-scaled in relation to its setting." Professor Simms believes that the castle has been beautifully restored by Dúchas and that the ramparts are in many ways the high-light for visitors. However from there, tourists "will look upon the flat roof of the hotel with all the modern apparatus of extractor fans etc. This view will detract from the visual appreciation of Trim Castle."

When describing the detrimental impact of the hotel on the town, Professor Simms says the hotel "dwarfs the charming terrace of Victorian cottages next to it which are protected structures."

"The architecture of the hotel is completely out of tune with the scale of the medieval town. Based on the National Monuments Act I believe that because of its intrusive character in the immediate neighbourhood of one of the country's most important national monuments, the hotel should not have got permission to be built on that site," Professor Simms told the Centre for Public Inquiry.

Under the Trim Town Development Plan 2000 it states that "development in the vicinity of listed buildings will only be permitted where the character and setting of such buildings are not impaired by the proposals."

Pictured left to right;
Councillor Danny O'Brien, Dr. Mark Hennessy T.C.D. and Anngret Simms
November 2004

Professor Simms attacks the council for not adhering to the plan and for failing to fulfil their obligations.

"By adopting the plan the Council gave an undertaking that it would regulate private development in a manner consistent with the objectives stated in the plan. By giving planning permission for the four-storey hotel in the immediate vicinity of the castle it failed in its obligation as the hotel is detrimental to the character of the architectural conservation area and will compromise the historic fabric and morphology of the area," Professor Simms said.

Professor Simms expressed her incredulity at the decision by An Bord Pleanála in June last to increase the number of bedrooms and car parking spaces in the development and reiterated her belief that the hotel should not have been built on the grounds that it contradicts the National Monuments Act 1930 as amended in 2004 and the Conservation Policy and Objectives for the historic town in the Trim Town Development Plan.

"

# THE RESTORATION OF TRIM CASTLE

Trim Castle on the banks of the River Boyne is the largest Norman castle in Ireland. The castle is an intriguing complex of medieval buildings. They comprise a largely intact and unique Keep, two gatehouses, and distinctive ranges of curtain walls and the footings of an extensive "palace range" that still imposes on the town and surrounding countryside.

In the 13th century the castle was the capital of a lordship that extended from the Irish Sea to the River Shannon where many of the monuments of the Norman settlement still stand.

Below the castle the town is developing around its medieval core where long stretches of the medieval wall survive. In the vicinity of the castle are remains of the abbeys of the Augustinian Canons, Dominicans and the site of the Franciscan house and St Patrick's Cathedral, believed to be the site of the earliest church in Trim.

East of the town is Newtown Trim, a medieval borough with the ruins of the cathedral of S.S. Peter and Paul and its priory, on the banks of the River Boyne. Across a 15th century bridge are the ruins of a hospital of the Crutched Friars founded in the early years of the 13th century.

## HISTORY

Hugh de Lacy was granted the Lordship of Meath by King Henry II in 1172. Soon after his arrival in Trim, de Lacy built a wooden castle, the timber and earthwork castle described in the Song of Dermot and the Earl – a poem of the period.

Called to serve the king, de Lacy left one of his barons Hugh Tyrell in charge, but when Ruairi O'Connor, High King of Ireland, threatened to attack Tyrell abandoned the area and the castle was burned by the Irish chieftain.

By 1176, the stone Keep replaced the wooden fortifications. When Hugh de Lacy was killed at Durrow in 1186, the Walter, a minor waited to inherit his fathers estates until 1190. The Keep was extended in at least two more phases and remodeled in his lifetime. It became known as King John's Castle after a visit by the new English King who arrived in Trim in 1210.

The Meath estates passed to Walter's granddaughter Maud in 1241. She married Geoffrey de Geneville a favourite of Henry III. This was the beginning of a period of prosperity for Trim The Great Hall and the adjoining private apartments were constructed. In 1306 de Geneville's granddaughter, Joan, married Roger Mortimer the 1st Earl of March. Their descendants held Trim until Edmund the 5th Earl died in 1425.

Throughout the 15th and 16th centuries the castle was in the care of officials of the crown, and a number of parliaments were held in Trim. Richard of York established a mint in the castle in 1460.

Trim was taken for a short period by Thomas Fitzgerald during the rebellion against Henry VIII in 1534. Subsequent plans to garrison and improve the castle were not followed and the castle fell into decline.

During the wars of the 1640s the castle was captured on various occasions by the rival forces and it was eventually abandoned to Cromwell in 1649.

Though the buildings of Trim Castle were adapted to suit the military and domestic needs of its occupants much of its fabric has remained unchanged since the height of Anglo-Norman power in Ireland.

Trim Castle in August, 1954. Photo: The late Jim Bambury (OPW)
*Courtesy of Dept. of Environment, Heritage & Local Government*

## CONSERVATION WORK 1971-1976
*National Monuments Branch, Office of Public Works*

The conservation work that was carried out in the 1970s on the gatehouses and the curtain walls ended a perceptible deterioration in the fabric of the castle. The work was carried out with a minimum of intervention. The historic structural evidence was respected and left to future study. The archeological excavations revealed a section of the fosse associated with the original "Ringwork" fortification. The footings of some of the medieval buildings within the south walls were also uncovered and conserved. The artifacts recovered established a broad context of the era and an insight into the living and trading activity of the castle's occupants and builders. The results of the excavation were published in 1978. (Proceedings of the Royal Irish Academy C Vol)

The scale of the 1970s project work could not be extended to the Keep though the castle grounds were made safe for casual visitors.

## CONSERVATION WORK 1991-1993

In 1991 the conservation of the Keep was undertaken along with a program of monitoring the work with a detailed recording the existing fabric.

The wall walks were sealed in concrete in the 1890s. This limited the effects of the weather and contained erosion of masonry. A similar but less intrusive treatment of the wall tops seemed suitable and was carried out with the stabilisation of the vaulting of the upper window embrasures. Extensive renewal of the battlements that were slighted by the garrison when they abandoned the castle in the 1640s was considered inappropriate. A conservation program was guided through decisions on the treatment of historic defacement, natural erosion and the scars left by absent fabric was encountered early in the project. An understanding and interpretation of the structure highlighted the need for research and comparative studies running in conjunction with the survey.

The stone of Trim Castle is a distinctive gray brown calp (limestone shale.) Repairs were limited by the availability of retrieved stone. Lime mortars were prepared and on site.

## DATED TIMBERS

Fifteen samples were taken from timber remains found in put-lock holes in the Keep. They were examined and felling dates were established. The dates relate to three main phases of activity in the 1170s, 1190s and in the early years of the 13th century. The function of these timbers was identified as the remains of scaffolding and hoardings and the timbers were left in-situ.

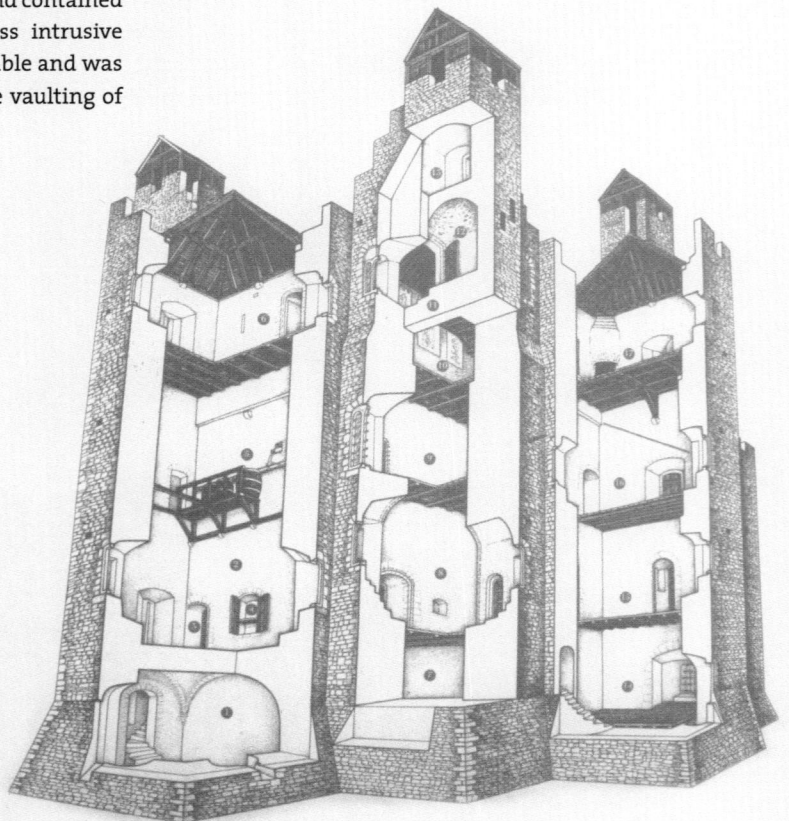

Trim Castle – The Keep

# SCOPE OF THE PROJECT EXTENDED
## 1993

In 1993 the castle was purchased by the state and increased funding was allocated to the project. A consultative group was commissioned to review the project. This is the part of the project undertaken by Gibney Architects. They looked at the provision of visitor services and at ways of linking the monuments in the town and made a general assessment of the impact of urban development.

While the work on site proceeded, the project was reassessed to allow full access to visitors without compromising the conservation principles that had been established. The story of the multi-phased development of the Keep was to be highlighted. The provision for access stairways and galleries would enable the appreciation of the Keep as a ruin, and allow the discontinued medieval structural history to be preserved and sealed.

The arrangements for public access required an external stair. Further archeological excavations were carried out below the entrance doorway high above the ground level in the east tower. The excavation examined the vicinity of the Keep and the extent of the "ringwork" discovered in 1972. The extensive remains of fore-buildings below the entrance to the Keep were discovered.

The line of the riverside curtain wall was excavated. The masonry had been almost entirely robbed over the years. Between the Mint Tower and the Great Hall the footings of a series of buildings were unearthed. They were identified as a small aisled hall replaced by the 15th century metal workshops. A blocked gate in the curtain wall and a passage leading to the undercroft of the great hall were also discovered. The footings of the hall were uncovered and the adjoining "Magdalene Tower", the remains of the 14th century residential apartments, was cleared. All the masonry remains were conserved and are presented to visitors.

While the works continued the design of a public access system began. The floors of the side towers were reinstated and bridges spanned the central block, linked the towers and provide dramatic internal views of the Keep. The structural strength of steel and wood was judged to be the best option to minimise the visual impact of the bridges. The external stairway was built on the footings of a masonry stairway. Built to comply with modern standards the steel and wood stairway rises to the entrance level and spans a drawbridge pit discovered by the archaeologists.

Tensioned fabric (P.T.F.E) canopies were installed to cover the Keep. Their profiles mimic the original roofs. Their visual impact was assessed by temporary installations and the least intrusive internal form and framework was considered. The canopy acts as a weather barrier preventing further water and frost damage to the Keep. Year round accessibility to the Keep is a major advantage of this intervention.

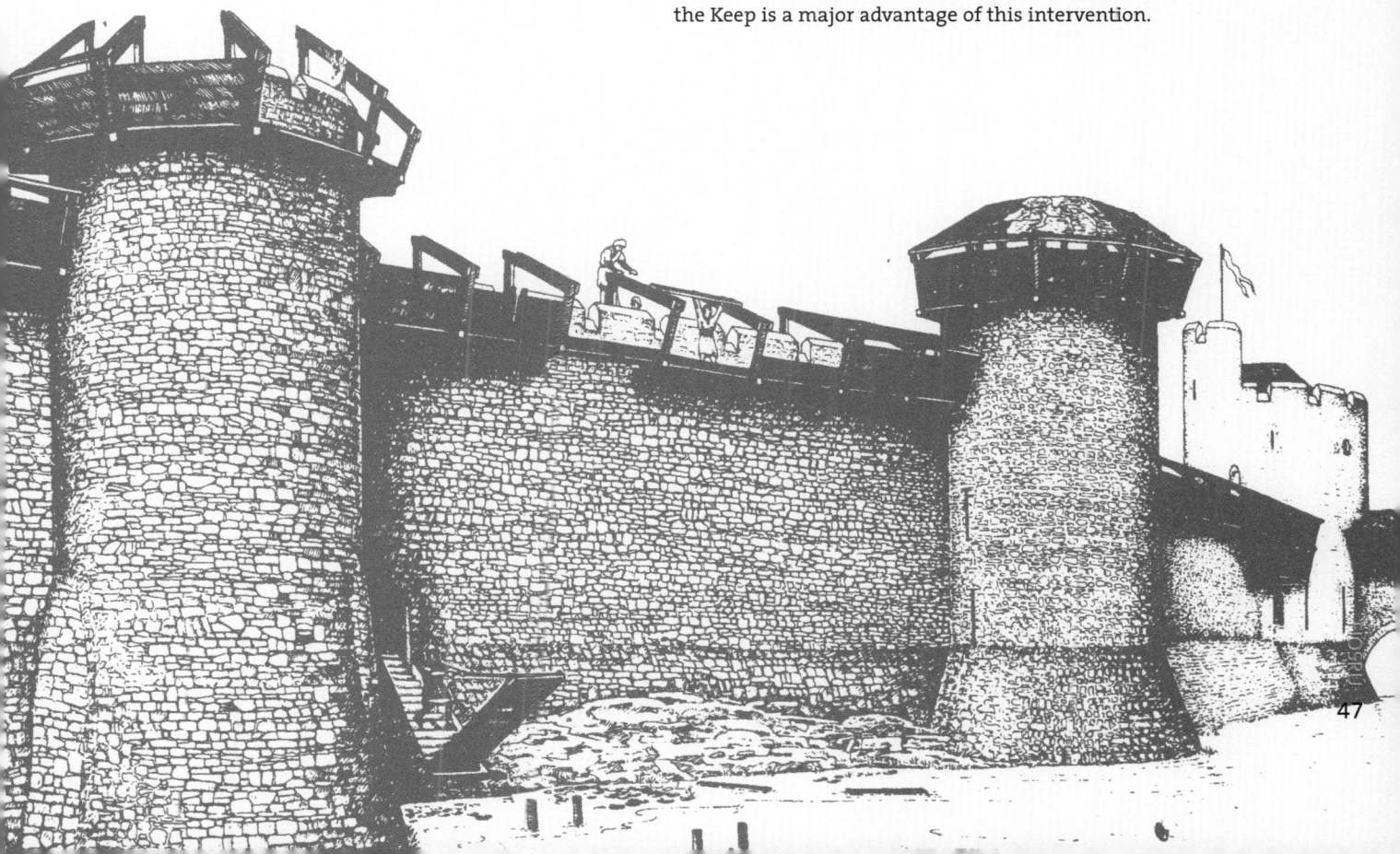

## WINDOWS

Most of the sandstone dressings of the door and window surrounds are absent. Many of the large opes, or openings, required barriers. The aim was to reduce ingress of wind and rain and discourage nesting birds while allowing sufficient ventilation to prevent condensation from the canopy. A strong fibre fine mesh framed and finished with a black coating was fixed to the internal opts and this proved to be effective and visually neutral.

Lighting was a major part of the project. Spot-lighting was used to pick up features of the castle's external walls while safety was the prime concern of the internal lighting.

The guide service accommodation was built within the ruins of the Trim Gatehouse. It was built as a freestanding box on two levels beneath the vaulted ceiling of the gaol. The fabric of the gatehouse was not altered.

## INTERPRETATION.

Visitors to Trim Castle are offered a guided tour of the Keep where large-scale models recreate the three main building phases of the Keep. A guidebook, leaflet and illustrated panels on the site provide information on the bailey and the outer curtain walls.

# TRIM CASTLE CHRONOLOGY

**1993**
The Office of Public Works acquires Trim Castle from Lord Dunsany.

**1994**
Arthur Gibney & Partners completes a development plan for the castle and its environs taking into consideration the implications for planning in Trim. One of the recommendations is to provide more car parking in the area for tourists.

**1995**
Archaeological excavations began around the Castle. Restoration work also commences.

**December 1996**
Brady Shipman Martin Planning Consultants are commissioned by Meath County Council and Trim Town Council to produce proposals identifying future expansion of the town centre including the new street link between Castle Street and Emmet Street in Trim.

**1997**
OPW agrees to pay £50,000 (€63,486) towards purchase and development of car park. Nuns' garden is sold to Trim UDC for £42,500.

**1998**
Sile de Valera confirms to Noel Dempsey that £3.0 from EU funds including £0.05m for car/bus parking is to go to the Trim Castle project.

**1999**
Variation to Trim Development Plan is approved to rezone areas to facilitate commercial development.

**2000**
A total of €4,469,514 was spent on restoring the Castle.

**March 2001**
A feasibility study commissioned by Meath County Council is prepared by Hassett Ducatez Architects. One of the points made in the report was that a large medium scale hotel would not be sustainable at this site although a small scale hostel accommodation could be provided.

**April 2001**
Advertisement is posted in the Meath Chronicle newspaper inviting developers to express interest in the development at the site on Castle Street.

**June 2001**
Bidders Conference takes place. Adjudication or advisory panel established to consider applications.

**December 2001**
Developers go before the adjudication panel. D. O'Brien Developments Ltd is awarded the tender and is so informed by Trim Town Council.

**March 2002**
Trim Development Plan 2002 adopted by Meath County Council. Includes need to preserve view from St Patrick's Church to Trim Castle. (See page 42 of Trim Development Plan, Views and Prospects.)

**May 2002**
Councillors challenge Town Manager Oliver Perkins at a meeting of the UDC as to how the decision was reached by the adjudication panel which some members claim had only an advisory role. Council property is sold to David O'Brien's company.

**February 2003**
D. O'Brien Developments Ltd puts in an application for a 4 storey hotel development with 68 bedrooms on the car park site.

**March 2003**
Dermot Kelly, Senior Inspector with An Bord Pleanála objects to the development.

**March 2003**
Robert O'Grady from the Development Application Section in Dúchas writes to Trim Town Council expressing concern with the scale of the development and requested further drawings and photomontages.

**April 2003**
Trim Town Council writes to Christopher Flynn & Associates acting on behalf of the developer requesting a revised design that would lower the Castle Street elevation and set back the top floor several metres and would show a 4.5-5 metre building free buffer zone between the proposal and the Church and the garden to the south east.

**April 2003**
A memo is sent to Wendy Moffett, Senior Executive Planner from Aidan Collins, Executive Planner. He

recommends that the fourth floor be set back several metres and that a 4.5-5 buffer zone be required between the hotel and the church. Although the planning application outlined 176 car park spaces, Collins believes that there should be 292. He also recommends a Visual Impact Assessment.

**May 2003**
Archaeological Impact Statement is completed.

**May 2003**
Development team meets with Dúchas representatives to discuss the development.

**June 2003**
Robert O'Grady in Dúchas sends a letter to Christopher Flynn & Associates which was copied to Aidan Collins. The letter states that while part of the upper floors had been pulled back in the revised drawings, Dúchas is concerned with a four-storey high corner that still remains.

**June 2003**
Flynn & Associates sends on further information to Trim Town Council in the form of plans and pictures. In the revised plans they reduce the number of bedrooms from 68 to 63. The revisions also include alterations to the 2nd floor and 3rd floor.

**July 2003**
Cllr Danny O'Brien sends a letter to Trim Town Council expressing concern with the development.

**July 2003**
The case is put on the List of Cases for Ministerial Approval by the Minister for the Environment, Martin Cullen. Treasa Langford from the Development Applications Section of Dúchas expresses concerns over the scale of the development. Despite having looked at revised plans (pulling back the floors as agreed on the 15 May at a meeting with the development team) and despite further revisions, Dúchas still believes that the development will have an adverse effect on the monument.

**July 2003**
Flynn & Associates send a letter to Trim Town Council informing them that they have removed bedrooms 30-36. This reduces the total of number of bedrooms to 58.

**July 2003**
Feargal O'Coigligh policy co-ordinator to the Minister sends an email to Treasa Langford referring to the Ministerial List. He informs Ms Langford that the Department should not recommend refusal of the development but that it be scaled back and he refers to revised plans prepared by the developer in this regard.

**August 2003**
Feargal O'Coigligh emails Liam O'Connell, Principal Officer with Dúchas saying that the appropriate response from the Department is not to refuse the development but to request that it be scaled back.

**August 2003**
Under a Manager's Order, D. O'Brien Developments Ltd. is granted permission for the 4 storey hotel with 58 bedrooms subject to 28 conditions.

**September 2003**
Pauline Gleeson and her colleague Brian Duffy senior archaeologist Dúchas draft a letter for An Bord Pleanála appealing the decision to grant permission by Trim Town Council on the grounds that the development is in the zone of archaeological potential and is subject to statutory protection in the Record of Monuments and Places, established under section 12 of the National Monuments (Amendment) Act 1994.

**September 2003**
Dermot Kelly writes to An Bord Pleanála appealing the decision of the 27 August made by Trim Town Council. His appeal is co-signed by Councillor Philip Cantwell and UCD Professor of Historical Geography, Anngret Simms.

**October 2003**
Kevin Mulligan from An Taisce submits observations in respect of the appeal to An Bord Pleanála. In the letter An Taisce supports the appeal of Dermot Kelly a planning inspector with An Bord Pleanála acting in a private capacity.

**October 2003**
Simon Clear, Planning and Development Consultant acting on behalf of the developer writes a lengthy letter to An Bord Pleanála defending the scheme and arguing that as an inspector with An Bord the objector, Mr Kelly, faces a potential conflict of interest.

**November 2003**
Dermot Kelly withdraws his appeal.

**November 2003**
Trim Town Council notifies the developer that permission is granted.

**November 2004**

Trim Town Council receives a further planning application from O'Brien seeking an additional 12 bedrooms and 54 car park spaces.

**November 2004**

Europa Nostra writes to newly appointed Minister for the Environment, Dick Roche, requesting him to review his predecessor Mr Cullen's decision not to appeal the decision to An Bord Pleanála.

**November 2004**

A press release from Europa Nostra requests a full review of the planning decision and requests that ongoing construction be halted until a compromise agreement for the development of the site had been reached.

**December 2004**

Dick Roche writes to Sean Foley from Trim Heritage Group stating that the £50,000 granted to the UDC for the purchase of the nuns' garden is under examination.

**January 2005**

Senior planning official, Aidan Collins recommends that planning permission be granted for the new application to increase the number of bedrooms and car parking spaces.

**January 2005**

Under a Manager's Order Oliver Perkins grants permission for the alterations to the hotel development pending two conditions that the applicant adhere to the original conditions under the earlier permission and that the development is in accordance with the plans submitted on the 10 November 2004.

**June 2005**

An Bord Pleanála upholds the planning permission subject to a number of conditions including the removal of two bedrooms reducing the number to 68.

Proposals impede view from St Patrick's Church to Trim Castle which according to the Trim Development Plan 2002 was to be preserved.

**24 August 2005**

Kevin Stewart, Trim Town Manager, writes to councillors informing them that the £50,000 grant for the car park given in 2000 will be refunded to the Department within a matter of days.

**25 August 2005**

Five councillors object to refunding the money until Department officials brief them of their reasons for such a decision.

**6 September 2005**

A meeting between councillors and Department officials takes place. The Manager explains to the councillors that he has the final decision with regard to returning the money.

**12 September 2005**

EU officials confirm that they are investigating a complaint that Environmental Impact Assessment procedures were breached in the planning process for the hotel development.

# Executive Summary

■ Serious concerns have been raised over the manner in which Trim Town Council disposed of land, in October 2002, to a developer to build a 68 bedroom hotel in the environs of Trim Castle, County Meath.

■ Members of Trim Town Council have claimed that they were persuaded, against their better judgement, to vote for the disposal of land to D.O'Brien Developments Ltd. who is building a hotel on the site at Castle Street.

■ An agreement was made between Dúchas and the local council for this site to be converted into a car park for visitors to Trim and the general public and Dúchas provided £50,000 for the development of this site. However the council decided to rezone the land and failed to inform elected members of their arrangement with Dúchas.

■ Local elected members were led to believe that an Advisory Panel would recommend a suitable tender for the rezoned land at Castle Street but that they, as members, would make the final decision. It was not until after the council had awarded the tender to David O'Brien Developments were the elected members informed that a decision had been made by the Panel. No public record exists as to how the tenders were assessed by the Advisory/Adjudication Panel.

■ A Senior Inspector with An Bord Pleanála objected to the hotel development but after stringent representations to An Bord Pleanála by architects acting for the developer, he withdrew his appeal.

■ The former Minister for the Environment, Martin Cullen, ignored advice from senior heritage officials who expressed, on several occasions, their deep objections with the development of a 4 storey hotel so close to Trim Castle, a significant national monument.

■ Despite the Minister's promises that the development would be scaled back, the hotel development today is equivalent to the initial planning application comprising of 68 bedrooms.

■ The Department of Environment has asked for the repayment of the £50,000 (€63,486) grant given to the local authority by Dúchas for the purchase of lands intended for a public car park in 2000. Despite objections by a number of councillors Trim Town manager, Kevin Stewart, has told the members that he intends to refund the money in order to maintain good relations with the Department.

■ The EU Environment Commission has launched an investigation into possible breaches of EU directives following a complaint that no Environmental Impact Assessment was carried out into the effect of the hotel development on Trim Castle.

■ Trim Castle was restored at a cost of €4.46m of which €3.8m was provided by the EU.